Drawing History

ANCIENT EGYPT

Elaine Raphael & Don Bolognese

SCHOLASTIC INC.

New York   Toronto   London   Auckland   Sydney

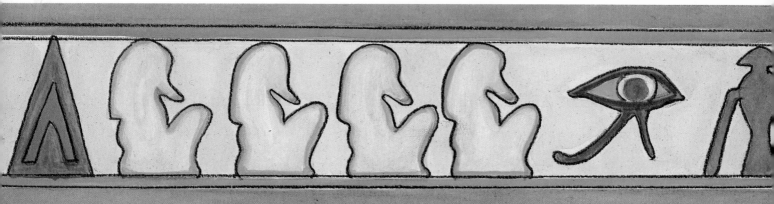

Contents

ISBN 0-590-48082-0

12 11 10 9 8 7 6 5 4 3   5 6 7 8 9/9

Printed in the U.S.A.   08

First Scholastic printing, September 1994

Introduction

Have you ever wondered how we know so much about life in ancient Egypt and other old civilizations?

During the last 150 years archeologists have uncovered the ruins of many ancient cultures. These discoveries have given us many clues about life in ancient times. And most of these clues have come in the form of art: wall paintings, sculpture, decorated bowls, clay tablets with writing, and personal jewelry.

In Egypt many works of art were discovered in the tombs and temples of Ancient Egypt. Because of their belief in life after death Egyptians filled their tombs with objects and paintings that reflected everyday life. For ancient Egyptians all of this was done out of religious faith. For us, the tombs are the best kind of history book; they make history exciting. Scenes of planting, harvesting, processions, warfare, and celebrations make it easy to imagine life 3,500 years ago along the banks of the Nile. And drawing those scenes of life in ancient Egypt will make the golden age of the Pharaohs seem even more real to you.

Getting Started

This book is a guide to ancient Egyptian history and ancient Egyptian art.

The illustrations were influenced by the art found in the Pharaohs' tombs. We used similar colors and the figure drawings resemble those done by the Egyptians.

However, there are two ways in which the drawings in this book are different from authentic Egyptian art. First, Egyptian paintings always showed the human face in side view. Second, Egyptian artists never used perspective to show space or shading to show three-dimensional forms.

We used both frontal and three-quarter views of the face (see pages 6, 15, and 17). To illustrate space we used perspective (see pages 10, 15, and 26), and almost all the paintings have some form of shading.

If you want to know more about ancient Egyptian art there are many beautiful books available. And perhaps you can visit one of the many museums with collections of paintings and sculpture.

Some hints to help you with all the drawing in the book.

All you need to get started on the drawings are pencil and paper.

Later, if you want to try painting, use any kind of watercolor paint and brushes. You should have at least one brush small enough to paint the detailed areas on the costumes and jewelry.

1. Before beginning a drawing take a few minutes and look carefully at the picture you are drawing. Look especially at its proportions. When you start, draw guidelines before sketching the figure. For chairs and other such objects use a ruler.
2. Are the basic proportions of your drawing okay? If so, the next thing you will need to do is to strengthen the outlines of your figure. Erase the unnecessary guidelines. Now put in the features with a sharp pencil.
3. Before you put in the finishing touches (jewelry, headdresses, costume patterns, etc.), look at your drawing and compare it to what you are drawing from. If something about your drawing

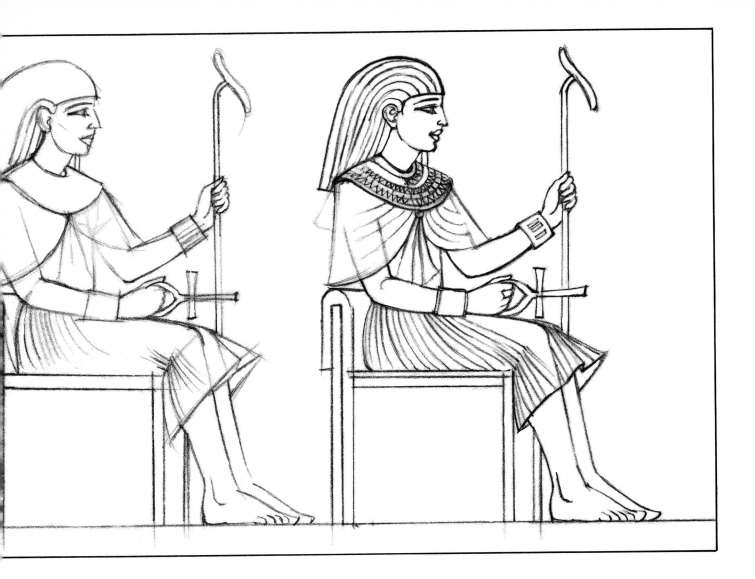

bothers you, don't do anything right away. Put the drawing away for a while, even for a whole day. When you compare your drawing and the original again, check the basic proportions first. If that's okay look at the features. Maybe they are out of line or the wrong size. After you've discovered and corrected what bothers you, then add the final touches.

Painting

If you want to paint one of your drawings, you first should transfer it to heavier paper. An easy way to transfer drawings is to rub the underside of your finished drawing with a soft (3B-4B) pencil. Place the drawing over the heavier paper and then trace the drawing with a very sharp pencil.

If you are using watercolors, paint the lighter colors first and add the dark ones after. Be sure to keep your colors clear and bright. After painting, you can outline areas with a very dark pencil. Instead of paint, you could also add color to the drawings in other ways: color pencils, markers, or even crayons.

The Pharaoh

The Pharaoh was the supreme ruler of ancient Egypt. He ruled over all the land and people in Egypt. As the head of their religion he was considered to be the human form of Horus, the falcon-god.

Here the Pharaoh is wearing the double crown of Egypt. This is a symbol of the two kingdoms of Upper Egypt (white crown) and Lower Egypt (red crown), which were united in 3200 B.C.

In his crossed arms Pharaoh holds two important royal symbols, the flail and a crook, also called a scepter.

The Pharaoh's godlike nature is represented by the priest, who wears the headdress of the falcon-god Horus and carries a scepter and the Ankh, the ancient Egyptian symbol of life.

The servant holds a golden bowl, a gift from one of the many nations that paid tribute to the great Pharaoh.

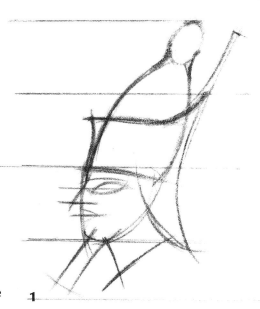

1

1. The crown is in two parts. The outer crown is shaped like a round pot. The inner crown is shaped like a bottle and fits into the outer crown. Draw these two basic shapes first. Add the head, which is only about half the size of the crown.
2. Add the details and features. Notice how the crown fits exactly around the Pharaoh's ears.
3. Begin the shading about halfway between the front and back of the crown. Note that the shadow is darkest where it begins and gradually lightens toward the back.

2

3

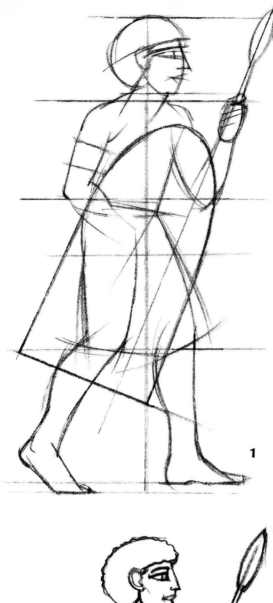

1. The foot soldier of ancient Egypt carried only a spear and an oxhide shield. The shield covered the area between the shoulder and the knee. Follow the horizontal guidelines for proportions and the vertical line for positioning the feet.

2. Add the features. Erase the guidelines that show through the shield. Draw shapes on the shield to make it look like an oxhide. Use a ruler to draw the spear shaft. A little shading down one side of the shield makes it rounder.

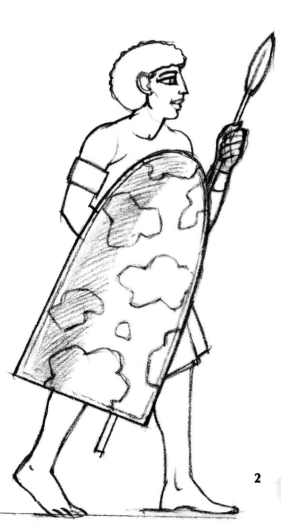

The Warrior King

The Pharaohs of ancient Egypt personally led their armies into battle. Their subjects expected them to be brave and fearless warriors. From his youth a Pharaoh was trained in the art of warfare. He was, for example, trained in archery and could hit a target from a moving chariot.

The Egyptian Army was made up mostly of foot soldiers. They were armed with spears and bows and arrows. Their wooden oxhide-covered shields were their only protection.

The charioteers were noblemen, who considered it an honor to fight at the Pharaoh's side. They, too, had to be skilled, because chariots, although frightening to the enemy, were very difficult to control and frequently turned over.

The Queen—Preparation for Court

In ancient Egypt the queen was very important. Her handmaidens and servants spent hours preparing her for public appearances. Royal jewelry and headdresses were not only beautiful, they had religious meaning as well. Here the queen is wearing a golden headdress representing the vulture-goddess Nekhbet.

Makeup and perfumed oils were applied generously not only because the Egyptians thought it was attractive but also to protect the skin in the hot, dry Egyptian climate.

On the queen's lap is a cat. Egyptians were fond of cats. They believed the cat was very important and considered it a sacred animal of Bastet, the lioness-headed or cat-headed goddess. Egyptian women so admired the cat that they made up their eyes to look like cat eyes. Cats were favored in an Egyptian household.

1. Keep the front paws and the hind feet on the same line so the figure sits firmly on the ground. Sketch the features, the tail, and the ears lightly.

2. Make sure you are pleased with the basic position of the figure and the placement of the features before you darken the outlines.

3. Add details like the collar and the earring (an especially Egyptian touch). Put in whiskers and shading to suggest the texture of fur.

Hunting and Fishing

The marshlands that bordered the Nile were rich with water-fowl, fish, and plant life.

Ancient Egyptian families like this one hunted and fished in the marshes for food and recreation. The father is aiming his throwing stick at a target somewhere among the papyrus reeds. Perhaps it is a heron like the decoy he is holding.

The young boy is carrying fish that he has just speared. Meanwhile his mother collects lotus flowers that she will use to decorate herself and her house. The family's two pets do their jobs, too. The goose acts as a decoy to attract wild geese, while the cat looks for ducks hiding among the water plants.

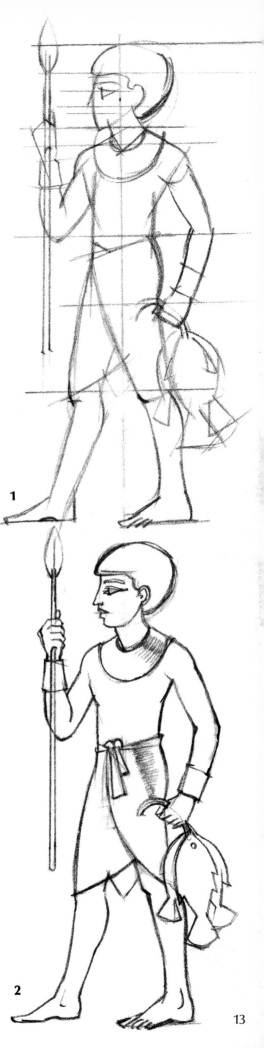

1. **Follow the guidelines for basic proportions. The boy's garment is called a kilt (like the skirt worn by men in Scotland). It ties around the waist and fits closely over the hips and thighs. Drawing the wide collar will help you get the right width on the shoulders.**

2. **Notice how the hands enclose the spear handle and the string of fish. In figure drawing, don't be afraid to emphasize elbows and knees. This will help your drawings of arms and legs look like bone instead of rubber.**

Farms Along the Nile

Ancient Egypt is often called "The Gift of the Nile." The Nile River provided water and topsoil for the farms of Egypt. Every summer when the Nile overflowed its banks, it spread rich black earth over the sandy soil. As the flood waters slowly receded, farmers worked the soil and planted seed. Several months later the

1. **Carrying a basket on one's head requires good balance. Keep the girl's back, shoulders, and head straight (follow the guidelines).**
2. **Most Egyptian dresses were form-fitting, so body lines are seen very clearly. Notice that the dress has a strap over only one shoulder.**

crops of wheat, barley, and vegetables were ready for harvest.

Here a young girl leads a donkey loaded with stalks of wheat to the threshing place. There the grains of wheat will be gathered and stored in granaries. All the crops belonged to the Pharaoh, who distributed them to his people.

Hieroglyphs and Scribes

Hieroglyphics, a form of writing in which pictures stood for letters of the Egyptian alphabet, developed in ancient Egypt around 3200 B.C. This form of writing was used on monuments and wall paintings. Another form called hieratic was for everyday use such as record-keeping. This is what the scribe is writing with his reed pen.

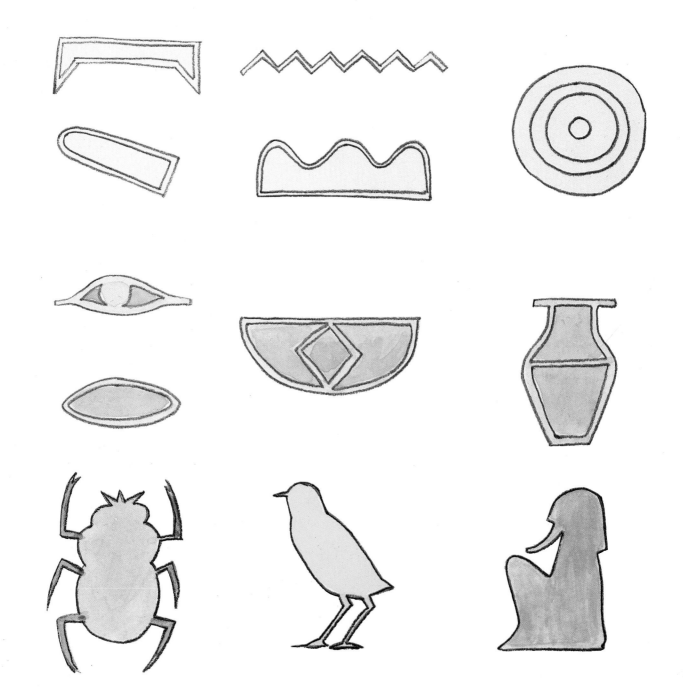

These are only a few of the hundreds of hieroglyphic signs that the scribes drew and painted on the walls of tombs. Sometimes the hieroglyphs were painted directly, while at other times they were first outlined and then filled in with colors or carved into stone. When drawing hieroglyphics, keep the outline clear. Don't draw tiny details or let the shape become too complicated.

The scribe's work was one of the most honored professions of ancient Egypt. Everyone, from the Pharaoh to the simplest farmer, depended on the scribes' skill at reading and writing. Education, trade between nations, and the preparations for the Pharaoh's tomb were all in the hands of the scribes. Here a scribe records the weight of gold rings sent to the Pharaoh from a conquered nation.

Painters of the Tombs

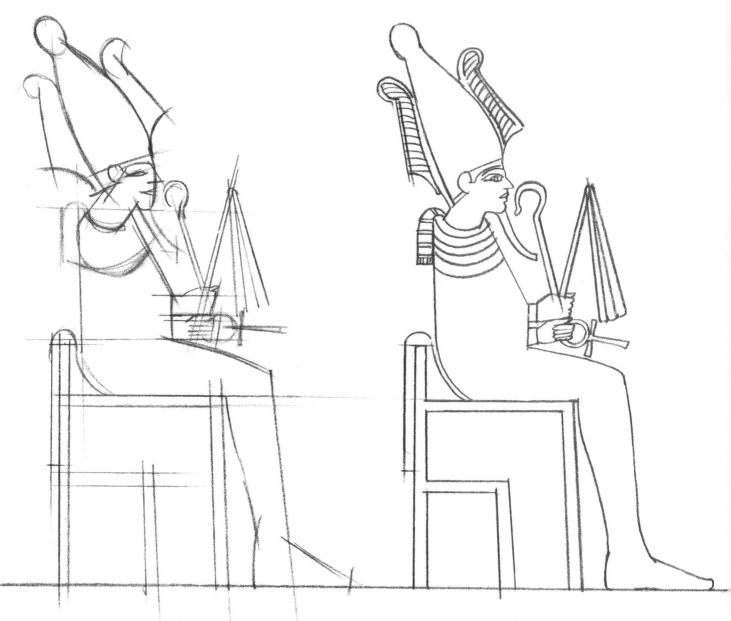

1. **This drawing is copied from a tomb painting. Notice how simply the figure is drawn. Everything is in profile (side view). To get clean, crisp lines use a ruler.**

2. **Add the details after you have sketched the basic figure (check the proportions). The finished outline drawing is perfect for trying a painting in the Egyptian style (just as the tomb painter is doing).**

The artists of ancient Egypt spent months and even years decorating a Pharaoh's tomb. The artists were skilled and respected craftsmen who began their apprenticeship as young boys keeping the draftsmen and painters well supplied with brushes and paint. Here a painter puts the finishing touches on a painting of a god.

In the foreground are art supplies and rolls of papyrus containing designs for the artist to follow. On the chest along the wall is an oil lamp, the artist's only source of light in the windowless tomb.

Mummification

Preparing a mummy took many weeks. All the work was done at a special place called the House of the Dead. The process began with the removal of the body's inner organs such as the liver and the lungs. They were preserved separately and put into canopic jars for burial alongside the mummy's coffin.

The body itself was completely drained of all its fluids and chemicals were added to it. After about seventy days the mummification process was finished. The body was then wrapped in linen and put into the coffin or tomb. All of these procedures were supervised by priests.

Here a priest, wearing the headdress of the jackal-headed god Anubis, says prayers over the mummy before it is taken to its final resting place in the tomb.

1. When you draw the canopic jar think of a cookie jar, one with a big, thick lid. Sketch the jar so that it looks hollow (see the circular guidelines). Add ears and a nose to the lid.

2. Define the features on the lid. Strengthen the outline of the jar and erase the circular guidelines.

3. To emphasize the jar's roundness add shading along one side. Add more darkness to the features.

1

2

3

Burial Rite

There were many ceremonies in the burial ritual. This one, "the opening of the mouth," was one of the most important. It was supposed to give life back to the dead person and insure the return of the "Ka" to the body. Once again Anubis, the god of the dead, is present. He holds the mummy upright while a priest recites the appropriate prayers.

1. A mummy case is symmetrical. Here is a simple method of making your drawing the same on both sides. On tracing paper draw a long rectangle. Divide it in half, lengthwise. Then sketch in a curved headpiece. Add the rest of the mummy case. Work on only one side of the case. When you are finished with one outline, fold the tracing paper along the dividing line and trace the finished side. This drawing will be on the underside of the tracing paper when you unfold it.

2. Flatten out the paper. The two sides of the mummy case should be exactly alike. Put a clean piece of tracing paper over the first and trace what you've already done. On this drawing, sketch in features.

3. Add curved lines to make the case round. These are also guidelines for adding hieroglyphs and other decorations. Strengthen outlines and features. Finally, add shading to make the mummy case even rounder in appearance (see the canopic jar and the Pharaoh's crown).

Boats on the Nile

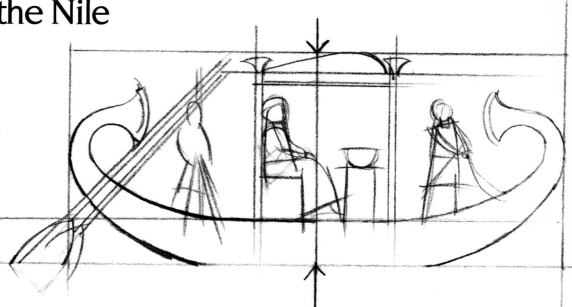

1. This boat is symmetrical. Use the same method to draw it that was used to draw the mummy case. The curved ends of the boat are very graceful.

The Nile was very important to ancient Egyptians. When a person died his or her mummy was carried by boat to the burial tomb. One oarsman at the stern of the boat controlled it with two oars.

On its final journey the mummy was accompanied by mourners. Here one kneels beside the coffin shaking ashes over her head, while another holds her hands before her face in a sign of sorrow.

2. After you have completed both ends of the boat add detail to the canopy. This boat is like the painted one (below) but carries live passengers instead of mummies. Follow the painted boat for decorations and details.

The Sphinx and the Pyramids

1. **With a ruler, draw this pyramid so that two of the sides can be seen. This view shows the pyramid as seen from ground level. A little shading on the right side makes it appear more solid.**

2. **The same pyramid as seen from slightly above ground level.**

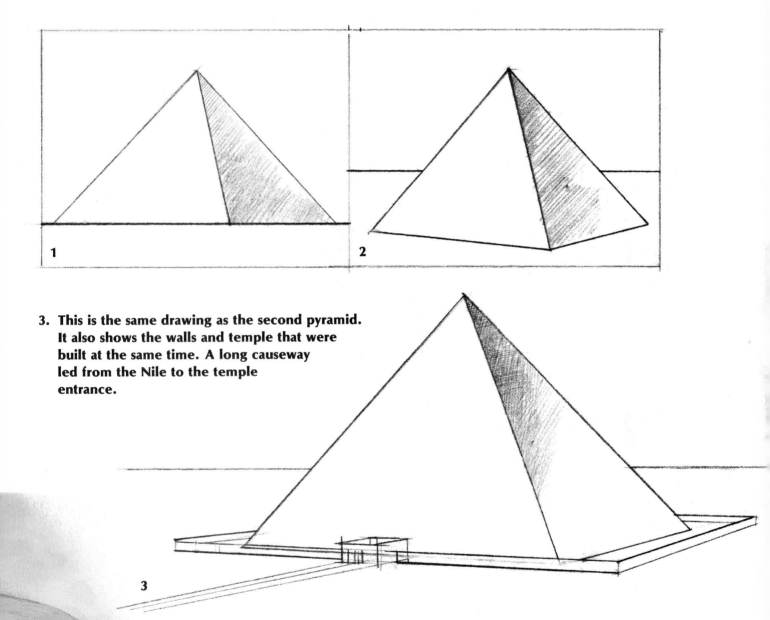

3. **This is the same drawing as the second pyramid. It also shows the walls and temple that were built at the same time. A long causeway led from the Nile to the temple entrance.**

The pyramids and the Great Sphinx of Giza, with the body of a lion and the head of a Pharaoh, are the most famous symbols of ancient Egypt.

The pyramids of the Old Kingdom were built as burial tombs for the Pharaohs of the fourth dynasty (2600 B.C.). The Great Sphinx was carved out of solid rock in honor of the Pharaoh. Here the Sphinx is shown as it might have looked then. Experts tell us that ancient sculpture was usually painted, although most of it has worn away over the centuries.

King Tutankhamen

In November 1922, after years of searching, a British archeological team led by Lord Carnarvon and Howard Carter discovered King Tutankhamen's tomb. It had been broken into by robbers years before, but surprisingly little had been taken. Most important, the burial chamber containing the coffin was untouched.

The contents of the tomb have taught us much about ancient Egypt. These objects are also among the finest examples of Egyptian craft work ever found. And perhaps the most powerful and beautiful of these is the king's golden mask. The mask covered the mummy's head and shoulders and is considered to be a likeness of the young Pharaoh.

1. Use the tracing paper fold-over method to draw the mask. Sketch in the complete mask but only outline one side. Fold the drawing in half and trace the outlined side. (See boat and mummy case.)

2. On the second piece of tracing paper trace the first outlined drawing. Leave out all the guidelines. Add details and darken areas like the eyebrows and beard. Now experiment with shading. Here's a good technique for trying something without ruining your drawing. Put a clean piece of tracing paper over the finished drawing. Put the shaded tones on the paper. If it looks good then do it on the full drawing.

Egypt in Ancient Times

Before 3200 B.C. the people of Egypt lived in small villages. Each village probably had its own ruler and religion. Over a period of time neighboring villages joined together to form larger communities. By 3200 B.C. there were two kingdoms: Upper Egypt (or southern Egypt) and Lower Egypt (or northern Egypt).

After 3200 B.C. a king from Upper Egypt called Menes conquered the Lower Kingdom and made Egypt one country. Its capital city was Memphis. During this period the writing we know as hieroglyphics was developed, and the civilization we call ancient Egypt began. The time from about 2800 B.C. to 2200 B.C. is called the Old Kingdom. It was a time of great wealth and prosperity, and produced two of the world's most famous monuments: the Great Pyramid at Giza and the Great Sphinx.

After two centuries of unrest and civil wars the Middle Kingdom began (2050 B.C. to 1650 B.C.) and the new capital city was Thebes. Toward the later part of this period a tribe called the Hyksos invaded Egypt. They brought with them the horse and the chariot. The Egyptians saw the military advantages of the horse-drawn chariot and began using it in their army.

In the New Kingdom (from about 1550 B.C. to 1100 B.C.) the Egyptians enlarged their empire. It was also the time of some very famous rulers such as Ramses II and Amenophis IV and his wife, Nefertiti. The monuments of Luxor and Karnak, which were to become famous, were built during this era. But, perhaps the most well-known relic of the New Kingdom is the tomb of Tutankhamen.

After 1000 B.C. Egypt suffered a series of invasions from other nations: first the Persians, then the Greeks, and finally the Romans dominated ancient Egypt.

Glossary

Ankh A cross with a loop at the top; the Egyptian symbol of life.

Anubis The jackal-headed god of the dead.

Archeologist A person who studies ancient civilizations.

Bastet A goddess with the head of a cat; the goddess of joy, music and dancing.

Canopic jar A jar for preserving and storing the insides of a body.

Causeway A raised roadway.

Flail A tool for threshing grain by hand.

Granaries Buildings for storing grain.

Hieratic A simpler form of hieroglyphics.

Hieroglyph A picture or symbol used by the Egyptians as an alphabet.

Horus The hawk-headed god of day.

Ka The double or soul of a person supposed to exist in a statue.

Lotus A flowering water plant.

Mongoose A small, weasel-like animal that attacks and kills poisonous snakes.

Mummy A body that has been embalmed and preserved for burial.

Nekhbet The vulture-goddess.

Papyrus A tall, grasslike plant that grows along the Nile River.

Pharaoh The title of the rulers of ancient Egypt.

Pyramid A large tomb with four triangular sides that meet in a point at the top.

Scepter A staff that is a symbol of kings.

Scribe A person whose job is to read, write, and keep records.

Sphinx A mythical creature with a lion's body and a human head.

Symmetrical Referring to an object or figure whose two halves are exactly alike.

Index